An Overview of World Finance

Contents

Chapter 1 A Survey of the World Bank
1.1 The Origin of the World Bank
1.2 The World Bank Group
1.2.1 The International Bank for Reconstruction and Development (IBRD)
1.2.2 The Other Four Institutions
1.3 The Articles of Agreement of the Bank
Chapter 2 The Evolution of the World Bank
2.1 The Early Years: 1946-1949
2.2 Financing Economic Development: Trickle-Down, Industrialization and Infrastructure 1947-1973
2.3 A New Style Lending Policy: Basic Needs and Redistribution with Growth 1973—1980
2.4 Adjustment Lending and Policy-Based Dialogue: 1980-Present
Chapter 3 An Overview of the World Bank
3.1 Organizational Structure and Operational Process of the World Bank
3.1.1 Membership and Financial Resources
3.1.2 Decision Making
3.1.3 Lending Policy
3.1.4 Steps of Obtaining a World Bank Loan
3.2 Activities of the World Bank
3.2.1 Financial Operations
3.2.2 Technical Assistance and Other Activities
Chapter 4 Appraisal by the World Bank

4.1　Technical
4.2　Institutional
4.3　Economic
4.4　Financial
Chapter 5　The Bank's Focus on Poverty
5.1　Introduction
5.2　Policy Changes at the World Bank
5.3　From Efficiency to Poverty Alleviation
5.4　Structural Adjustment Lending
5.5　From Structural Adjustment to Fighting Poverty
5.6　Poverty and Environment
5.7　Put People First
5.8　Dedicate Staff Resources to Fighting Poverty
5.9　Towards an Anti-Poverty Strategy
5.10　Mobilize Adequate Financial Resources
5.11　Conclusion
Chapter 6　The World Bank and International Environmental Agenda
6.1　Introduction
6.2　New Initiatives
6.3　Causes of Environmental Degradation
6.4　Sustainable Development
6.5　Focus of Criticism
6.6　Conclusion
Chapter 7　Innovation of the World Bank's Work and Challenges Ahead
7.1　Innovative Work of the World Bank
7.2　Challenges Ahead
Chapter 8　The World Bank in the New Century
Appendix:　The World Bank in China

Chapter 1

A Survey of the World Bank

1. 1   The Origins of the World Bank

Early plans for the IBRD date back to 1942. The idea was to establish two financial institutions to be owned jointly by the countries of the world. The first, the IMF, would be concerned primarily with the stability of currencies and the correction of disturbances in the balances of payments of its members. The second, the IBRD, would help reconstruct war-damaged economies and generally promote growth in less-developed member countries. Both would foster international trade and progressive improvement in global standards of living.

Like the IMF, the World Bank was created at Bretton Woods in July, 1944, the culmination of wartime discussions between the United States and the United Kingdom on the shape of the post-World War II international economic order. The IMF was established to provide funds for short-term balance of payments relief and the role of the International Bank for Reconstruction and Development was the provision of longer-term finance for the development of productive resources. The initial priority of the IBRD, which opened for business on 25 June 1946, was reconstruction.

The Bank that emerged from the Bretton Woods conference was mainly conceived in terms of the economic problems of the immediate post-war period. It was the tasks of reconstruction rather than the challenge of development which ranked uppermost in the minds of its major proponents. The developing countries attending the conference were concerned that if too high a priority was placed on reconstruction, limited resources would be available for development. The Latin American countries therefore proposed that in the Articles of Agreement equal emphasis should be given to reconstruction and development. The United States conceded the inclusion of development functions in the Articles of Agreement so that Latin American countries would agree to join the IMF. Nevertheless, the provision of capital for reconstruction of the war-damaged economies dominated the concerns of the organization in the first years.

The founders of the Bank, i. e. the United States, the United Kingdom and other delegations at Bretton Woods were strongly influenced by the experience of international lending in the 1920s and 1930s. During the interwar period capital raised through the sale of securities in foreign capital markets had frequently been put to unproductive purposes and had made little or no contribution to the productive capacity of the borrowers. Many loans had been made at high interest rates without reference to the ability of borrowers to service new or even existing foreign debt In the light of these considerations certain safeguards were built into Bank lending. First loans are made only for productive purposes and except in special circumstances only for specific projects. Secondly, the Bank only lends to governments or enterprises guaranteed by a member government, central bank or comparable agency. Thirdly, the Bank's loans are not tied, i.e. no conditions are attached to where they can be spent. Fourthly, the Bank is a lender of the last resort

The Bank only lends if it is satisfied that the borrower is unable to obtain finance from private sources under reasonable conditions.

1.2 The World Bank Group

1.2.1 The International Bank for Reconstruction and Development (IBRD)

The IBRD itself became operational in 1946. It was conceived by the U.S. Government in the early years of the Second World War as one of two pillars of the world economic system in the postwar era, the other being the International Monetary Fund (IMF). And as the World Bank Group's leading organization, the World Bank was established along with the International Monetary Fund at the Bretton Woods, New Hampshire, conference held in 1944 by United Nations members for the purpose of forming the lead financial agencies of the United Nations. It was originally established to make loans to member governments for the purpose of post-World War II reconstruction and for development of poor member countries. Its current activities are limited to economic development loans and related programs for developing member countries.

Loans made or guaranteed by the IBRD were to finance "specific projects" — except in special circumstances and to be financed mainly by funds that the institution borrowed from the market. The new inter-governmental bank was, however, expected primarily to be a facilitator of foreign private capital flows (as a guarantor of and participant in foreign private loans) and a supplementary source of direct financing when such private loans were not otherwise available on reasonable terms. Ten billion

U.S. gold dollars made up the initial authorized capital of this Bank. While its members included 38 countries in the first year, its earliest operations were limited to a few European countries.

The IBRD has since greatly outgrown the dreams of its architects and early advocates. It operates now in developing countries where per capita income and the general level of development are low enough to justify IBRD support but where the countries are nevertheless deemed to be able to service their debt to the IBRD. The financing of specific projects is still required to be the main business of the IBRD in normal circumstances, but this has been broadly understood to cover loans and guarantees for any well-defined productive purpose in the economic or social fields. The exception of ' general purpose lending' in special circumstances has also been used liberally since the beginning of the eighties, and loans for structural and sectoral adjustment have reached 29 percent of total operations in 1989. These loans have been made mainly to governments or to government-owned agencies and corporations (the Bank is legally required to obtain a government guarantee if the borrower is not the government of the member).

1.2.2 The Other Four Institutions

The International Finance Corporation (IFC) was established in 1956 as an affiliate of the World Bank. Its members must be members of the World Bank. It makes private-sector investments, rather than loans to governments.

The International Development Association (IDA) was established as an affiliate of the World Bank in 1962. This agency makes infrastructure loans to the lowest income developing countries on the same basis as the World Bank, only with government guarantee.

The World Bank also sponsors two other agencies that, although they do not make loans, are very import institutions. These are ICSID and MIGA, and one of the major objectives of each of them is to encourage the flow of foreign private investment into the lowest-income developing countries.

The International Centre for Settlement of Investment Disputes (ICSID) was established in 1966. It facilitates the arbitration of contract disputes when one party is a foreign investor from a country that is a member of ICSID and other party is the host state government also a member of ICSID.

The Multilateral Investment Guarantee Agency (MIGA) is a relatively young organization, which began operations in 1988. This agency insures foreign investment in member countries against the political risks of violence such as war or revolution, expropriation of property, interference with contractual obligations, and restrictions on the use of local currency.

Like IBRD, the common objective of these organizations is to help raise the standard of living in developing countries by channeling financial resources from developed countries to developing regions.

During the years since the Bretton Woods Conference, the Bank and its affiliates have continued to develop in response to the changing needs of their members. They now offer new and more effective methods for achieving economic development, through the provision of technical as well as financial assistance to the developing world. In view of the enormous gap between developed and developing nations, and after so many years in which the world neglected these problems, it seems unrealistic to expect the Bank to have been more successful in the short term, although hopefully its efforts will bear fruit in the long term. For the immediate future, it seems that the Bank will remain the leading agency for assistance to the developing countries, and will continue its support for their efforts at economic and institutional reform.

1.3   The Articles of Agreement of the Bank

The IBRD s Articles of Agreement were amended effective December 17, 1965 and February 16, 1989. Article I lists the Bank's purposes:

(i) To assist in the reconstruction and development of territories of members by facilitating the investment of capital for productive purposes, including the restoration of economies destroyed or disrupted by war.........

(ii) To promote private foreign investment by means of guarantees or participations in loans and other investments made by private investors.....

(iii) To promote the long range balanced growth of international trade and the maintenance of equilibrium in balances of payments by encouraging international investment for the development of the productive resources of members ......

(iv) To arrange loans made or guaranteed by it in relation to international loans through other channels so that the more useful and urgent projects, ... will be dealt with first.

(v) To conduct its operations with due regard to the effect of international investment on business conditions in the territories of members.........

Article II covers membership in and capital of the Bank. Section I states that membership is open to all members of the International Monetary Fund. Subsequent sections cover the authorized capital of the Bank; subscription of shares; issue price of shares; division and calls of subscribed capital; limitation on liability; method of payment of subscriptions; time of payment; the maintenance of value of certain currency holdings of the Bank; and restrictions on disposal of shares.

Article III contains general provisions relating to Bank loans and guarantees, including use of the Bank's resources; dealings between members and the Bank; limitations on guarantees and borrowings by the Bank; conditions on which the Bank may guarantee or make loans; and loans to the International Finance Corporation (IFC). This Article was amended December 17, 1965 to enable the Bank to "make, participate in, or guarantee loans" to the Corporation, for use in its lending operations.

Article IV describes the Bank's operations. The various sections cover methods of making or facilitating loans; availability and transferability of currencies; provision of currencies and payment provisions for direct loans; guarantees; the Bank's special reserve; and methods of meeting Bank liabilities in case of default. The concluding section prohibits interference by the Bank and its officers in the political affairs of any member, "nor shall they be influenced in their decisions by the political character of the member or members concerned".

Article V covers the organization and management of the Bank. Section one, "Structure of the Bank' states that "The Bank shall have a Board of Governors, Executive Directors, a President, and other officers and staff to perform such duties as the Bank may determine".

Section Two is devoted to the Board of Governors, in which "all the powers of the Bank shall be vested' The Board consists of one Governor and one alternate appointed by each member country. A Bank Governor is usually the member country's minister of finance, a governor of its central bank, or equivalent. The Board meets annually, and its meeting is held in conjunction with the annual meeting of the Board of Governors of the International Monetary Fund.

Section Three covers voting. In both the Bank and the IMF a weighted system has been adopted. Each member has two hundred and fifty votes plus one additional vote for each share of Bank stock held. These share holdings are calculated according to members' quotas in the IMF, and are based on their financial situation, so that richer countries subscribe to more shares than Third World countries. This variable allotment of shares recognizes the differences among members' holdings, and is intended to protect the interests of those countries that make a larger contribution to the Bank's financial resources.

Section Four describes the functions of the Bank's Executive Directors, who are responsible for the conduct of the general operations of the Bank. There are 24 Executive Directors, working on a full-time basis at the Bank's headquarters in Washington, D. C.. Five of the Directors are appointed by the five members with the largest holdings of the Bank's capital stock; the remainder are elected by Governors representing groups of the other countries. The President of the Bank is also chairman of the Executive Board. The President, subject to the general control of the Executive Directors, is responsible for the organization, appointment, and dismissal of the Bank's officers and staff and is also required, subject to the paramount importance of securing the highest standards of efficiency and of technical competence' to recruit personnel on as wide a geographical basis as possible. Traditionally, since the establishment of the Bank and the Fund, the President of the Bank has been an American, and the Managing Director of the IMF a European.

Section Five is devoted to the Advisory Council, appointed by the Board of Governors, which advises the Bank on matters of general policy. The remaining sections cover the Bank s loan committees; relationships with other international organizations; location of Bank offices; regional offices and councils; depositories; holdings of currency; publication of reports; and allocation of net income.

Article VI deals with withdrawal and suspension of membership, and suspension of operations and settlement of Bank obligations; and Article VD covers the Bank's status, immunities and privileges. Article VIII contains "Amendments", and describes the procedures to be adopted when modifications to the Articles of Agreement are proposed. This Article was amended in February 1989, so that proposed amendments to the Articles of Agreement would require acceptance by members with four-fifths of the total voting power. Article IX covers interpretation of the provisions of the Articles of Agreement; Article X includes "Approval deemed given" by member countries; and Article XI contains "Final provisions".

Chapter 2

The Evolution of the World Bank

From its inception until present, the growth and development of Bank activities can be analyzed in four periods. This periodisation is based on the dominant approach to development and, the focus of the Bank's lending. In the first period (1946--1949) the Bank's main interest was in reconstruction. The second phase (1949--1973) is coterminous with the financial and organizational expansion of the institution from the IBRD to the World Bank Group. In this period the Bank concentrated on promoting industrialization. The third phase (1973 –1979) saw an expansion in bank lending and a new emphasis on the rural sector. The fourth phase (1980--present) is dominated by adjustment lending and a greater role for program lending. The McNamara years are normally viewed as a specific chapter in the Bank's history reflecting both his dominant personality and imprint on the institution and the movement away from the dominant economic strategy of the previous era. But in the first five years of McNamara's presidency, the Bank's orientation was similar to that under the previous president, George Woods, and the move to adjustment lending was made before he stepped down from office.

2.1 The Early Years: 1946 -- 1949

No loans were distributed in 1946, although loan

applications were made by several countries. Eugene Meyer the first president spent the period trying to gain the confidence of the financial community. After repeated conflicts with the US Executive Director Meyer resigned in December 1946. The new president, John J. McCloy, presided over the first four loans totaling $497 million, extended to Denmark, France, Luxembourg and the Netherlands in 1947. These were program loans and it was not until the following year that the Bank made its first project loan. This loan, to Chilli, signaled the major form Bank lending took over the next three decades. By 1947 it was apparent that the Bank's resources were inadequate to cope with the demands of West European reconstruction. With the launch of the Marshall Plan the Bank's role in financing reconstruction was effectively over. It continued to supply financial resources to European countries, particularly to southern Europe, but by 1953 of a total disbursement of $1.8 million, roughly $1.0 million was for development projects located outside Europe. The reorientation of the bank s activities towards its poorer clients began at an early stage in its history. When McCloy resigned the leadership in May 1949, his statement that 'the reconstruction phase of the Bank's activity is largely over', was correct but his observation that the development phase….is under way, was somewhat premature. It was under the presidency of Eugene Black (1949-1962) that the Bank made the decisive shift to financing economic development.

2.2 Financing Economic Development: Trickle-Down, Industrialization and Infrastructure 1947-1973

This second phase saw the Bank expand its lending and develop a specific approach to economic development. Under Eugene Black s leadership the Bank successfully transformed itself from a focus on reconstruction to one on development. Lending policy was heavily influenced by the prevailing theories of development. The dominant development paradigm perceived underdevelopment to be the result of low savings, high population growth and a series of bottlenecks in the local economy. Development and growth were used interchangeably and it was believed that the successful pursuit of economic growth would lead to development. The path to growth was through industrialization and the development of infrastructure. With this theoretical underpinning Bank lending concentrated on economic growth-related projects. Investment was targeted to sectors such as infrastructure, transportation and energy. A combination of investment in these sectors, financial stability and sound monetary and fiscal policies provided the key to development according to this perspective. The sectoral allocation of Bank lending between 1949-1963 gives a clear indication of the Bank's priorities. Until 1963, the 73.7 per cent of Bank lending was allocated to infrastructure (communications, power and transportation). And between 1961 and 1965, the 76.8 per cent of all Bank lending went to electrical power and transportation.

This period also witnessed an increase in the activities of the World Bank. Loans increased from $137.1 million in 1949 to $1,332.4 million in 1965 but fell back to $953.6 million in 1968. Increased lending was partly a consequence of the organizational expansion of the IBRD. In 1968, for example, IDA credits accounted for $106.6

million of the total mentioned above. To finance the new lending the Bank capital was increased, in 1959 from $10 million to $21 million.

Moreover, the IFC provided extra assistance to the private sector. In its first five years of operation its commitments were about $18 million per year but under the presidency of George Woods (1963-1968), IFC commitments grew to over $50 million in 1967--1968. Bank aid to the private sector was also expanded through the use of development finance companies (DFCs). Bank lending to DFCs in this period was larger than its IFC commitments. For example, in 1966, lending to DFCs reached $100 million and increased to $159 million in 1968.

Important though it was to channel funds to the private sector through the IFC and DFCs, it was the creation of the IDA in 1960 which best embodies both the expansion of the Bank and its firm commitment to economic development. Writing in 1971, Robert Asher noted that "The creation of the IDA can be considered as a major milestone in the as-yet-incomplete transformation of the World Bank Group into a development agency." The creation of the IDA with its favorable lending conditions enabled the World Bank to reach out to countries unable to afford the tougher IBRD loans and to increase lending to previously neglected sectors like agriculture and education.

Other innovations during this period included the establishment of an Economic Development Institute in 1955 to provide short-term training for administrators in developing countries and the development of a Technical Assistance Program to assist borrowing countries in the preparation of loan applications and development plans.

The expansion of the IBRD into the World Bank Group arose partly as a result of the pressures exerted by the developing countries in the UN system in the 1950s. Dissatisfaction with the international economic system led to demands for a Special United Nations Fund for Economic Development (SUNFED). The Third World's quest for increased concessional financial aid was answered by the creation of the IFC and IDA. Western nations rejected the SUNFED concept but compromised by expanding the operational role of an organization they controlled. In the early part of its second phase, the Bank successfully responded to the wave of decolonisation through institutional expansion but retained its largely conservative lending principles.

In 1968 the World Bank acquired a new president who began to make changes that would eventually lead the Bank to abandon the trickle-down theory. Some of the most dramatic changes in Bank direction took place under the leadership of Robert McNamara (1968--1981). During the McNamara presidency, the Bank dramatically increased its lending and developed a new focus on poverty alleviation. It also became a more high profile and controversial organization as it attempted to grapple with rapid change in the international economic system. This period witnessed the end of the stable exchange rate system established at Bretton Woods, the end of the post-war economic boom, the onset of recession and the oil price rises of 1973-1974 and 1979. Most developing countries faced a hostile and unpredictable international economic climate for most of the 1970s. The relative stability of the post-war-economic system was shattered by rising inflation, a downturn in economic activity in the major industrial centres and increased turbulence in the international economic system. This unfavorable economic climate coincided with the frustrations felt at the poor results of the First Development Decade (1961-1970). The launch of the Second Development Decade seemed an act of despair rather than one of hope. The failure of Third World development strategies, increased economic insecurity and the possibility of increased influence due to the possession of commodity power led to a demand, in 1973, for a radical restructuring of the international economic order. The changes of the World Bank in the 1970s have to be placed in the context of failed Third World development, a turbulent international economic environment and the concerted pressure of the G77 and NAM for the creation of a New International Economic Order.

McNamara s first and most concrete change was to increase drastically the number and amount of loans and to shift the regional focus of lending. By 1969 World Bank financing had increased 87 per cent over the previous year and 86 per cent of all Bank spending up to 1981 occurred during McNamara's tenure. The number of projects also rose dramatically from 62 in 1968 to 266 in 1981 with equivalent costs of $953.5 million and $12.4 billion respectively. World Bank lending to Africa rose from $134.6 million to $2812.4 million, to Asia and the Middle East from $305.5 million to $5889.6 million and to Latin America from $385.5 million to $3153.2 million. In percentage terms, Africa's share increased from 16.3 per cent to 23.7 per cent, that of the Asian and Middle East region rose from 37 per cent to 49.6 per cent, and Latin America experienced a relative decline in flows from 46.7

per cent to 26.6 per cent.

2.3 A New Style Lending Policy: Basic Needs and Redistribution with Growth 1973 - 1980

McNamara's presidency will, however, probably best be remembered for reorienting the Bank away from the "trickle-down theory'. As Hurni put it, "the new style lending projects can be seen as an attempt to practice a 'trickle-up' strategy in order to help the poor without hurting the rich who generally produce more for their national economies and have higher savings and investment rates".

The idea of redistribution with growth became the dominant theoretical approach to development during this period. McNamara's famous policy speech in Nairobi in 1973 is frequently taken as the turning point in the Bank's new approach. But the 1973 speech, although important in generating political commitment and prioritizing rural development projects, echoed themes McNamara had been articulating soon after taking office. Ascher has suggested that the political importance of the Nairobi speech arises from a convergence between US policy-makers' rethinking of development and the World Bank's new approach.

McNamara committed the Bank to poverty-oriented projects because in his view, previous development efforts had failed to reach the absolute poor, defined as the bottom 40 per cent in developing countries. As noted in the Redistribution with Growth report, although the average per capita income of the Third World has increased by 50 per cent since 1960, this growth has been very unequally distributed among countries, regions within countries, and socioeconomic groups. The aim of the new approach was to raise income levels in developing countries without increasing income inequality or to raise income levels to a level which would lead to an improvement in income equality as a result. The new strategy consisted of two approaches. A basic-needs approach with a focus on investment in human capital and, to complement this an emphasis on rural development. It should be noted that the Bank was not the sole exponent, or indeed the pioneer, of the basic-needs approach to development. Other international organizations, notably the International Labour Organization (ILO), contributed significantly to the articulation of the basic-needs paradigm. After 1973, rural development became the main lending priority of the Bank. In fiscal year (FY) 1974, loans for rural development projects totaled $500 million but in FY 1979 this had risen to $2000 million.

This new emphasis on basic needs and rural development was reflected in the sectoral allocation of Bank spending. Agriculture and rural development represented only 18.1 per cent of Bank lending in 1968 but by 1981 it accounted for 31 per cent of the total. Nevertheless, in the context of overall Bank policy it is instructive to note that although the agriculture and rural development program received the largest share of Bank lending, taken together the traditional sectors of energy, transportation and telecommunications still accounted for the bulk of Bank lending.

The new policies were integrated with old concerns, i.e. funds were channeled to poverty-oriented new-style lending projects within the existing sectors. In agriculture, funds were shifted from infrastructural projects like irrigation to those concentrating on, for example, land settlement and agricultural credit. Between 1974 and 1978, approximately 75 percent of the 363 agricultural and rural development approved by the Bank contained a small farmer element or component. And over 50 per cent of Bank lending for agriculture and rural development between 1974--1978 went to projects in which more than half the direct benefits were expected to accrue to the rural poor.

Bank lending for education increased with a shift in resources to primary and non-formal education. Between 1979 and 1983, the 21.2 per cent and 24.6 per cent of Bank lending for education went to primary education and non-formal education respectively. Bank lending for urban poverty alleviation was developed and more emphasis given to health projects.

Internal reorganization of the Bank's bureaucracy was also undertaken to implement the reforms. New departments were created — Agriculture and Rural Development (1973), Urban Projects (1975) and Population, Health and Nutrition (1979). Furthermore, in 1976 a Project Preparation Facility was initiated to enable the poorest countries to plan and prepare projects capable of meeting the criteria laid down by the Bank.

During this period the Third World countries were concerned about the weighted voting system in the Bank and attempted to increase their influence in decision-making. The Bank was among a number of international organizations targeted for reform of their decision-making structures. It is not difficult to see why this campaign ended in failure. It is unlikely that the major shareholders in a financial institution are likely to agree to a decision-making formula which fails to distribute voting shares proportionately to paid-in capital.

The Third World also attempted to increase participation in the Bank through increased representation of their nationals on the Banks staff. The number of officials from developing countries increased during this period and the proportion of North Americans and Europeans on the Bank's professional staff fell.

2.4 Adjustment Lending and Policy-Based Dialogue: 1980-Present

It was the McNamara presidency which effectively ended the focus on basic needs. In his final year in office, the Bank initiated a new type of program lending. The structural adjustment loan (SAL), created in 1980, has been the focus of much current criticism of the Bank. The SAL was initiated in response to the deteriorating balance of payments position of a number of developing countries and reflected the desire of the top management in the Bank to exert greater control over the policy environment of Bank lending. The move to adjustment lending shifted the goal of the Bank's activities away from poverty alleviation to policy dialogue. The aim of SAL is to force developing countries to implement policy reforms devised by the Bank. Adjustment lending supports programs of specific policy changes and institutional reforms in order to achieve improvements in the balance of payments, maintain economic growth in the face of severe constraints and increase inflows of external assistance. The dominant motif of Bank lending in the 1980s and 1990s is policy dialogue or adjustment lending.

Three challenges have confronted the Bank in this period.

The onset of the debt crisis in 1982 brought increased demands on Bank resources from the heavily indebted middle-income developing countries. The Bank was slow to respond to this challenge and developed an active strategy only after James Baker, the US Secretary of State, in October 1985 proposed a central role for the Bank in debt management.

The catastrophic failure of development policies in Sub-Saharan Africa compounded by wars, famines and natural disasters with the attendant human and physical degradation, has drawn the attention of the world community to the dire plight of Africa s peoples. The Bank responded to the worsening situation in Africa with a series of special lending instruments and a commitment to increase the flow of financial resources to the continent. The revolutions in Eastern and Central Europe and the end of the Cold War expanded the Bank's membership and brought new clients in search of foreign aid.

In attempting to adapt to the financial needs of its poorer member states the Bank has once again been influenced by the leading ideas on economic development. The 1980s saw the triumph of economic conservatism in the industrialized countries and the forging of a new consensus on economic policy. The Bank's basic economic philosophy is biased in favor of market and private enterprise solutions. From the outset, Bank policy has been in favor of the free flow of goods and services across national boundaries. In the 1980s and 1990s the Bank has given greater support for neoliberal principles and the argument that market solutions are preferable to intervention. The international economic environment of the 1980s was an uncertain one. For many developing countries it was a period of negative growth with declining export prices, rising import prices, shrinking commercial lending and increased indebtedness. The recession in the industrial countries harmed the export prospects of many developing countries and rising protectionism shut them out of markets in which they were competitive.

The Bank began the 1980s on the defensive from attacks by its principal shareholder, the United States, and ended the decade trying to defend itself from accusations that it was a mere tool of Western interests. Its enhanced role in coordinating creditors' clubs and conditional lending gave it increased leverage over its poorer members and this fuelled the debate on its role in the Third World. The extent to which the bank pursues independent policies or is merely the instrument of its leading members is a contentious issue. But we can note at this point that the Bank has been a chosen instrument of the United States and its allies in the handling of the debt crisis and the reconstruction of the former communist states of Eastern Europe.

The Third World countries reacted anxiously to changes in Bank policy in the early 1980s. The move away from poverty alleviation was viewed with scepticism. Many saw the reassertion of conservative banking principles, e.g. co-financing, flexible interest rates and graduation, as signaling the retreat of the Bank from its role as a development agency. Nevertheless, the parlous economic circumstances in which the majority of developing countries found themselves led to calls for increased Bank assistance rather than less. For example, the Third World countries proposed that the Bank's gearing ratio be doubled to 2:1. They argued that the 1:1 ratio was too conservative and placed too severe a limit on the Bank's ability to raise capital. Third World governments were also against the increase in conditionality which was seen in some cases as an infringement of sovereignty.

Chapter 3

An Overview of the World Bank's Work

3.1 Organizational Structure and Operational Process of the World Bank

3.1.1 Membership and Financial Resources

The IBRD stands at the centre of the World Bank Group. Its membership has grown from 38 countries in 1946 to 180 at present. Membership of the IBRD is a prerequisite for membership of the IDA and IFC. It is owned by its shareholders, i.e. the 180 member countries. The Bank's capital structure is made up of authorized capital, callable capital and its own borrowings in the international bond markets. And it has other sources of funds including return on its loans, spinoffs of its loans to other financial institutions. Each member pays in one-tenth of their share capital creating a common liquidity pool of paid-in capital which finances the operations of the IBRD. The remaining

90 per cent of share capital is held by governments as callable capital and is subject to call if and when required to meet obligations of the IBRD arising out of borrowings or guarantees. This guarantee fund or reinsurance capital cannot be used for administrative purposes, it has never been called upon and is unlikely ever to be used. The capital structure is designed to provide the IBRD with substantial resources of its own and a large guarantee fund enabling it to mobilize private capital. The reserve of callable capital underwriting Bank borrowing gives Bank bonds first class status (a Triple A rating in the United States) in the countries where it borrows. Initially borrowing was restricted to the United States but now the Bank borrows in European and Japanese markets in addition to the US.

3.1.2 Decision Making

The highest decision-making organ in the IBRD is the Board of Governors. All members are represented on the Board of Governors which meets annually. Apart from certain important functions such as amending the Articles of Agreement or admitting new members, the Board has delegated its powers to the Executive Board. The Executive Board consists of 24 appointed and elected executive directors. The five largest shareholders appoint one director each and the others are elected every two years. Elected executive directors represent groupings of countries with some directors representing a constituency comprising both developed and developing states. The Executive Board operates on the basis of a weighted voting system with votes based on subscriptions to the IBRD. As at June 30, 1992 the five largest shareholders and their voting shares were the United States (17.59), Japan (8.01), Germany (6.19), France (5.93) and the United Kingdom (5.93). The smallest constituency consisting of 22 African states totaled 1.86 per cent of voting shares. Decisions are based on simple majority and this gives the major donor states, especially the United States, significant influence over Bank decisions. Recourse to formal voting, however, is rare, with most decisions based on consensus. But consensus should not be taken to imply either the absence of conflict or power in the decisional process. Influence is exercised in a more delicate fashion with the largest shareholder able to send signals of disapproval and so prevent issues from reaching the Executive Board.

The president of the Bank is the chairman of the Executive Board and exercises his/her vote only in the event of a tied vote. S/he is chief of the operating staff of the Bank and subject to the direction of the executive directors on questions of policy. S/he is responsible for the conduct of the ordinary business of the Bank, the organization of the staff and the appointment and dismissal of officers and employees. The Bank's management enjoys a relatively greater degree of autonomy than other international organizations. The autonomy of the management arises from a combination of the Bank's independent financial base, the impressive technical and intellectual reputation of its staff, its pre-eminent position among multilateral lending agencies and the activities of successive presidents to develop and preserve organizational autonomy.

3.1.3 Lending Policy

The lending policy of the Bank is governed by the Articles of Agreement which placed a ceiling on lending. The Bank is forbidden to lend over and above its subscribed capital, plus surplus and retained earnings. The Bank has a very conservative ratio of loans to capital and reserves of 1:1, and a similar high liquidity level with a debt equity ratio of 1:24 compared with a 20:1 ratio for commercial banks. The Bank was founded on sound financial principles and one reason for its high standing in the international financial community is the continuation of this careful and prudent approach. Thus the Bank is constrained not by its capacity to borrow but by the size of its subscribed capital and the restricted ratio of loans to capital. Bank loans are made below the prevailing commercial rates of interest.

Initially, apart from exceptional circumstances, the Bank lent almost entirely for specific projects but from the onset of the 1980s it has been heavily engaged in program lending. Bank lending is shaped by a number of factors and considerations pertaining to the importance of the project and the creditworthiness of the borrower. It is vital that the project has a high priority in the development program of the borrower and can show a financial and economic return. At the outset, the identification of projects was the sole responsibility of governments. Loans are made available only when other sources of finance on reasonable terms are not available. The role of the Bank is to assist in accelerating the time when the borrower will be able to raise funds in the international capital market. Moreover, as a lender of the last resort, the leverage the Bank can exert is thus greater than if the Bank was competing to finance projects with other agencies.

The Bank lends only to countries it regards as creditworthy. Assessment of creditworthiness is not based on any clearly defined criteria and is a mixture of economic analysis of the borrower's ability to repay and a psychological estimation of the borrower's willingness to repay debts. The economic criteria used to determine a borrower's credit status include debt service ratio, the total share of medium-term and long-term debt held by the Bank, increases in annual per capita GNP, savings and investment rates, balance of payments position and the openness of the economy. Assessment of a country's willingness to repay is based on a subjective evaluation of the past repayment record and current resolution of a borrower to give priority to the interests of foreign creditors. The Bank takes the "willingness to repay" criterion further and refuses to lend to countries in dispute with foreign private investors or official foreign governmental agencies. Disputes can arise from the nationalization of the assets of a foreign corporation without adequate and effective compensation, failure to honor agreements. e.g. over taxation with foreign private investors or default on debt repayments without agreement on refinancing. The Bank's not concerned with disputes involving domestic creditors. Bank lending is largely for the financing of the foreign exchange costs of projects and Bank, projects are subject to international competitive bidding.

3.1.4 Steps of Obtaining a World Bank Loan

Obtaining a World Bank loan is a lengthy process that involves six steps-identification, preparation, appraisal, negotiation, implementation and supervision, and evaluation. In the identification phase the borrowing country decides which project should be proposed with the help of the World Bank. This may take 1 to 2 years.

Preparation for the project will also take between 1 and 3 years and requires detailed analysis of all aspects of the project-technical, economic, financial, and social. Identification and preparation are the responsibilities of the borrowing country even though it may receive assistance from the IBRD. Appraisal of the project is done by the World Bank over a 3-to 6-month period. Rarely is the project rejected at this stage, but some modifications may be required. Once the project appraisal is completed, the Bank and the borrowing country enter into negotiations on the terms of project implementation. The negotiated conditions are documented in the loan agreement. This stage usually takes between 1 and 2 months. Project implementation is the responsibility of the borrowing country, but the IBRD does supervise both procurement of needed materials and project implementation. The implementation may require 6 years or more. Once the project is completed and the loan has been fully disbursed, the Word Bank performs an evaluation of the project, comparing the actual results with the anticipated results. The results of these evaluations are then published in the Bank's annual review of projects.

3.2   Activities of the World Bank
3. 2.1   Financial Operations
In the late 1940s and early 1950s, the Bank concentrated on reconstruction in Europe after the Second World War. When the war-damaged economies began to recover, the Bank was able to devote its resources to "the encouragement of the development of productive facilities and resources in less developed countries' as laid down in

Article 1 of its Articles of Agreement. The authorized capital stock of the Bank, originally fixed at US $10,000m but since increased to more than US$ 17.000m, consists of shares subscribed by its members. Their subscriptions are based on their quotas in the International Monetary Fund. Most of the Bank's funds for financing development are derived from its dealings in the international capital markets, including bond issues (which have a 'triple A" rating), from retained earnings, and from repayments of Bank loans. According to its Articles, 'the Bank may guarantee, participate in, or make loans to any member….". But its loans are made only to creditworthy developing country members, or repayment has to be guaranteed by the government concerned if it does not participate in the loan. The Bank's loans are made to finance productive investments in these countries when private capital is not available at reasonable rates. They are repayable within fifteen years or less, and usually have a five-year grace period. Before the Bank approves a loan, a Bank loan committee has to study the proposal and recommend acceptance. Because of all the safeguards attached to Bank loans, they are considered very safe investments, and have a catalytic effect in generating additional investment.

During the first phase of its development lending, from the 1950s to the mid-1960s, the Bank invested mainly in large-scale industrial and infrastructure projects involving the construction of power-plants, roads, railways, ports and dams. It was then believed that this type of investment was a prerequisite for successful development, and that its 'trickle-down' effects would benefit the whole population. However, in the 1960s, poverty in many African and Asian countries made it necessary to address the basic needs of the poorest people more directly.

Under the leadership of the Bank's fifth President, Robert S. McNamara, the Bank entered into the second phase of its lending for development. Its new objectives included redistribution with growth, which placed equal emphasis on economic growth and poverty alleviation, and satisfying the basic needs of the poorest people. Loans were made for integrated rural development projects in the agricultural sector, and for projects involving population planning, public health, water supply and sanitation, housing, and urban development. The rise in oil prices in the 1970s caused the Bank to increase its assistance to oil-importing developing countries. Changes were also made in the traditional areas of Bank lending, with more emphasis on the construction of rural roads in transportation projects, on power for rural areas in power projects, and on job creation and small enterprises in industrial projects. The Bank also supported the development of alternative forms of energy, including coal, gas, oil, wood, and biomass. During this phase of the Bank's activities, the new emphasis on poverty alleviation profoundly affected not only its lending policies, but also many of its assumptions about the development process, and made the Bank a leader in efforts to reduce poverty in the Third World.

A third phase of Bank lending began in 1980, with the introduction of the Bank's structural and sector adjustment loans. These were intended to assist developing countries to adjust their policies and restructure their economies while they attempted to achieve sustainable adjustment with growth. Such loans differed from the Bank's traditional project loans, because they were linked with reform programs rather than development projects, and were for shorter periods than project loans. Although Bank lending in this decade continued to be directed towards the achievement of sustainable economic growth and the reduction of poverty (During fiscal year 1993. the World Bank implemented one of its fundamental objectives, i.e., poverty reduction.) with special emphasis on sub-Saharan Africa, the Bank's new involvement in balance of payments adjustment caused policy disagreements with some borrowing countries, especially when the conditionality of Bank loans was tightened, and was more closely linked with political as well as economic liberalization policies.

An issue which assumed more importance for the Bank in the 1980s was the protection of the environment. Concern about the ecological effects of Bank projects had already been expressed in the previous decade, but it was not until the 1980s that the Bank established an environment department, and introduced comprehensive environmental assessment procedures into project design. In 1990, the Bank, together with the United Nations Development Program and the United Nations Environment Program, established the Global Environment Facility to assist developing countries in implementing projects that benefit the global environment as well as the individual country. The Bank administers this Facility, and is responsible for the implementation of investment projects.

3.2.2 Technical Assistance and Other Activities

In addition to its financial operations, the Bank provides

important technical assistance, training and research services. One of the most important parts of its technical assistance is the work done by Bank economic missions. At the request of a member country, a mission, consisting of a group of experts, visits the country to collect and analyze information about its economy, review government policies, and present policy recommendations. The reports of such missions not only form a basis for Bank assistance, but are also very valuable sources of current information about member countries, especially as they contain extensive statistical annexes with up-to-date statistics from the country itself as well as from the Bank's extensive collections. The Bank also undertakes sector and project analysis, and its loans may include funds for management or planning advice.

The provision of technical assistance to member countries has become a major component of Bank activities. The economic, sector and project analysis undertaken by the Bank in the normal course of its operations is the vehicle for considerable technical assistance. In addition, project loans and credits may include funds earmarked specifically for feasibility studies, resource surveys, management or planning advice, and training. Although the Bank finances technical assistance activities as part of a loan or credit or in the form of a grant, in some cases it urges the government requesting the assistance to approach the UNDP for funds (United Nations Development Program-UNDP, established in 1965 by the General Assembly to help the developing countries increase the wealth-producing capabilities of their natural and human resources.). Technical assistance is also extended to countries that do not need the Bank financial support.

Examples include short-term training; secondment of advisers; transfers of technology, such as computer expertise; serving on evaluation and monitoring panels; and providing demography, financial and economic advice for project preparation.

The Bank's Economic Development Institute (EDI), established in 1955, provides training courses in economic and project analysis and management for government officials from member countries. Courses are held at the Bank's headquarters in Washington. And also overseas, where the institute is attempting to build up local capacity to organize such courses. In addition, the institute produces training materials, organizes symposia and workshops, and is the administrator for a fellowship program and Bank graduate scholarships.

Research, undertaken by staff in the Bank's Research Department, supports Bank activities and policy advice, and is intended to encourage the development of research activities in member countries. Current Bank research includes human resource development; poverty alleviation; the environment, forestry, and natural resources; and macroeconomic issues such as adjustment, public finance, external debt, and trade, and the private and public sectors in development. In 1971, the World Bank, the Food and Agricultural Organization of the United Nations, and the United Nations Development Organization established the Consultative Group on International Agricultural Research (CGIAR) to support research for improving crops and animal, production in the developing countries. The Bank appoints the chairman of the Group, which includes governments, private foundations, and international agencies, provides offices for the Group's secretariat in

Washington, and makes a substantial contribution to its activities.

Chapter Four

Appraisal by the World Bank

As the project takes shape and studies near completion, the project is scheduled for appraisal. Appraisal, perhaps the best known phase of project work (in part, because it is the culmination of preparatory work), provides a comprehensive review of all aspects of the project and lays the foundation for their implementing the project and evaluating it when completed.

Appraisal is only the Bank's responsibility. It is conducted by Bank staff, sometimes supplemented by individual consultants, who usually spend three to four weeks in the field. If preparation has been done well, appraisal can be relatively straightforward; if not, a subsequent mission, or missions, to the country may be necessary to complete the job. Appraisal covers four major aspects of the project- technical, institutional, economic, and financial.

4.1 Technical

The Bank has to ensure that projects are soundly designed, appropriately engineered, and follow accepted agronomic, educational, or other standards. The appraisal mission looks into technical alternatives considered, solutions proposed, and expected results.

More concretely, technical appraisal is concerned with questions of physical scale, layout and location of facilities; what technology is to be used, including types of equipment or processes and their appropriateness to local conditions; what approach will be followed for the provision of services; how realistic implementation schedules are; and what the likelihood is of achieving expected levels of output. In a family planning project, the technical appraisal might be concerned with the number, design, and location of maternal and child health clinics and the appropriateness Of the services offered to the needs of the population being served: in highways, with the width and pavement of the roads in relation to expected traffic and the trade-offs between initial construction costs and recurrent cost for maintenance, and between more and less labor- intensive method of construction; in education, with whether the proposed curriculum and the number and layout of classrooms, laboratories, and other facilities are suited to the country's educational needs.

A critical part of technical appraisal is a review of the cost estimates and the engineering or other data on which they are based to determine whether they are accurate within an acceptable margin and whether allowances for physical contingencies and expected price increases during implementation are adequate. The technical appraisalalso reviews proposed procurement arrangements to make sure that the Bank's requirements are met. Procedures for obtaining engineering, architectural, or other professional services are examined, in addition, technical appraisal is concerned with estimating the costs operating project facilities and services and with the availability of necessary raw materials or other inputs. The potential impact of the project on the human and physical environment is examined to make sure that any adverse effect will be controlled or minimized.

4.2 Institutional

In the Bank's current terminology, institution building has become perhaps the most important purpose of Bank lending. This means that the transfer of financial resources and the construction of physical facilities. however valuable in their own right, are less important in the long run than the creation of a sound and viable local "institution", interpreted in its broadest sense to cover not only the borrowing entity itself, its organization, management, staffing, policies, and procedures, but also the whole array of government policies that conditions the environment in which the institution operates.

Experience indicates that insufficient attention to the institutional aspects of a project leads to problems during its implementation and operation. Institutional appraisal is concerned with a host of questions, such as whether the entity is properly organized and its management is adequate to do the job, whether local capabilities and initiative are being used effectively, and whether policy or institutional changes are required outside the entity to achieve project objectives.

These questions are important for traditional project entities; they are even more important (and difficult to answer) for the entities charged preparing and carrying out the new-style projects intended to benefit the rural and urban poor, where there may be no established institutional pattern to follow. The Bank's experience to date has not yielded any readymade solutions for putting together an institution that can effectively and economically deliver goods and services to large numbers of people-often in remote areas and outside the ordinary ambit of government-and that can motivate them and change their behavior.

Of all the aspects of a project institution building is perhaps the most difficult to come to grips with. In part, this is because its success depends so much on an understanding of the cultural environment.

4.3 Economic

Through cost-benefit analysis of alternative project designs, the one that contributes most to the development objectives of the country may be selected. This analysis is normally done in successive stages during project preparation, but appraisal is the point at which the final review and assessment are made.

During economic appraisal, the project is studied in its sectoral setting. The investment program for the sector, the strengths and weaknesses of public and private sectoral institutions, and key government policies are all examined.

In transportation, each appraisal considers the transportation system as a whole and its contribution to the country's economic development. A highway appraisal examines the relationship with competing modes of transport such as railways. Transport policies throughout the sector are reviewed and changes recommended, for example, in any regulatory practices that distort the allocation of traffic. In education, power and telecommunications, the "project" as defined by the Bank may embrace the investment program of the whole sector. Whenever the current state of the art permits, projects are subjected to a detailed analysis of their costs and benefits to the country, the result of which is usually expressed as an economic rate of return. This analysis often requires the solution of difficult problems, such as how to determine the physical consequences of the project and how to value them in terms of the development objectives of the country.

Over the years, the Bank has kept in close touch with progress in the methodology of economic appraisal.

"Shadow" prices are used routinely when true economic values of costs are not reflected in market prices as a result of various distortions, such as trade restrictions, taxes, or subsidies. These "shadow" price adjustments are made most frequently in the exchange rate and labor costs used in the calculations. The distribution of the benefits of a project and its fiscal impact are considered carefully, and the use of "social" price to give proper weight in the cost-benefit analysis to the government's objectives of improved income distribution and increased public savings is passing through an experimental phrase.

Less frequently, in cases of major uncertainty, a risk/probability analysis is also carried out. The optimal timing of the investment is tested in relation to the first year's benefits. When the Bank provides funds to intermediate agencies (developmental finance companies, agricultural credit institutions) for relending to smaller operations, or in the case of sector lending, those agencies own appraisal methods must be acceptable.

Some of the elements of project costs and benefits, such as pollution control, better health or education, or manpower training, may defy qualification; in other projects, for example, electric power or telecommunications, it may be necessary to use proxies such as revenues that do not fully measure the value of the services to the economy. In some cases, for example, education, alternatives are likely to involve different benefits as well as different costs, and a qualitative assessment must suffice. Whether qualitative or quantitative, the economic analysis always aims at assessing the contribution of the project to the development objectives of the country; this remains the basic criterion for project selection and appraisal. And while greater concern with the distributional effects of projects reflects broader objectives of development, it does not mean that the Bank has lowered its standards of appraisal. Whether "old" style or "new", every project must have a satisfactory economic return, and a standard that the Bank believes serves the best interests of both the country and the Bank itself.

4.4 Financial

Financial appraisal has several purposes. One is to ensure that there are sufficient funds to cove the costs of implementing the project. The Bank does not normally lend for all project costs; typically, it finances foreign exchange costs and expects the borrower or the government to meet some or all of the local costs. In addition, other co-financers, such as the European Development Fund, the several Arab funds, the regional development banks, bilateral aids, and a growing number of commercial banks, are joining to an increasing extent in financing projects that, in many instances, are appraised and supervised by the Bank. Therefore an important aspect of appraisal is to ensure that there is a financing plan that will make funds available to implement the project on schedule. When funds are to be provided by a government known to have difficulty in raising local revenues, special arrangements may be proposed, such as advance appropriations to a revolving fund or the earmarking of tax proceeds.

For a revenue-producing enterprise, financial appraisal is also concerned with financial viability. Will it be able to meet all its financial obligations, including debt service to the Bank? Will it be able to generate enough funds from internal resources to earn a reasonable rate of return on its assets and make a satisfactory contribution to its future capital requirements? The finances of the enterprise are closely reviewed through projections of the balance sheet, income statement, and cash flow. Where financial accounts are inadequate, a new accounting system may be established with technical assistance financed out of the loan.

The financial review often highlights the need to adjust the level and structure of prices charged by the enterprise. Whether they are publicly owned or not, enterprises assisted by the Bank generally provide basic services and come under close public scrutiny. Because the government may wish to subsidize such services to the consuming public as a matter of policy, or perhaps simply as the line of least resistance, it may be reluctant to approve the price increases necessary to meet its financial objectives. But adequate prices are a sine qua non of Bank lending to revenue-earning enterprises, and the question of rate adjustments may be critical to the appraisal and subsequent implementation of a project.

Financial appraisal is also concerned with recovering investment and operating costs from project beneficiaries. The Bank normally expects farmers to pay, over time and out of their increased production, all of the operating costs and at least a substantial part of the capital costs of, say, an irrigation project. Actual recovery in each case takes account of the income position of the beneficiaries and of particular system of charges or of levying higher charges on Bank-assisted projects than are collected elsewhere.

Costs can be recovered a variety of ways-by charges for irrigation water, through general taxation, or by requiring farmers to sell their crops to a government marketing agency at controlled prices. Some countries apply lower standards of cost recovery than those recommended by the Bank; thus, arriving at a common judgment on what is desirable and practicable can be one of the more difficult aspects of the appraisal and subsequent negotiation.

To ensure the efficient use of scarce capital, the Bank believes that interest charges to the ultimate beneficiaries should generally reflect the opportunity cost of money in the economy (indicating the cost of foregone alternatives). But interest rates are often subsidized, and the rate of inflation may even exceed the interest rate. In countries with high rates of inflation, a system indexed rates is sometimes followed. As in the case of cost recovery, the appropriate level of interest rates may be a contentious issue. The Bank may have to set its sights on a long-term goal, recognizing that it will take time to bring about what may be far-reaching changes in financial policy. This may be particularly so when the government is seeking to control interest rates and other prices as part of an anti-inflation program.

The appraisal mission prepares a report that sets forth its findings and recommends terms and conditions of the loan. This report is drafted and redrafted and carefully reviewed before the loan is approved by the management of the Bank for negotiations with the borrower. Because of the Bank's close involvement in identification and preparation, appraisal rarely results in rejection or designed during this process to correct flaws that otherwise might have led to its rejection.

Chapter 5

The Bank's Focus on Poverty

5.1 Introduction

Poverty must be a central concern of the World Bank. The essence of development is enabling people to be productive and to improve their levels of well-being. Whatever the Bank must do to enhance development should have the inevitable and ultimate effect of reducing poverty and strengthening the base for a higher standard of living.

After more than 50 years of operations, the Bank still faces a world where 1 billion people live in deep poverty, with per capita incomes of less than a dollar per day. Many countries suffer poverty rates between 25 and 50 per cent of their populations. These conditions persist despite important improvements in critical social indicators such as life expectancy, infant mortality, access to safe water, primary school enrollment and immunization. It is urgent that the Bank steps up lending to improve basic conditions through lowering population growth and strengthening primary education, sanitation, health and nutrition.

5.2 Policy Changes at the World Bank

Poverty eradication has proven to be an extremely complex task. In recent years these complexities have been underscored by several non-governmental organizations (NGOs) which have moved into the center of the debate about the Bank's role in fighting poverty. NGOs have also been involved in a number of critical policy changes that the bank introduced in the late 1980s, in particular

- ✧ Systematic attention to environmental issues in project and policy work, and the establishment of a Vice Presidency for Sustainable Development, including an Environment Department;
- ✧ Greater attention to the role of women in development; Greater attention to poverty issues that arose as a consequence of structural adjustment lending, especially in Sub-Saharan Africa (SSA), and the ensuing 'Poverty Reduction Program';
- ✧ Greater participation in project preparation and

implementation by people directly affected by these projects;
- ⟡ Establishment of the Inspection Panel to bring complaints about projects to the attention of Bank management and Executive Directors; and
- ⟡ Establishment of a public information center and increased availability of project and economic documents.

These and other changes have made the Bank an entirely different institution from what it was in 1985. Indeed, it is no exaggeration to say that the Bank has experienced an institutional revolution that is still in progress. In each one of these changes, NGO have pinpointed critical issues, persuaded the Bank to pay greater attention to them, and put pressure for appropriate policy change. Moreover, NGOs are working with Bank staff in repairing projects in the field. They also played a role in the formulation of programs to counteract the effects of structural adjustment lending on poverty. The extent of NGO involvement in Bank-financed projects has grown measurable since the late 1980s.

World Bank management and staff meet regularly with NGO representatives to explain Bank policy and to listen to comments to consider what action can be taken on them. However, NGOs, being more directly concerned with ethical issues and values and closely attuned to local culture and social conditions, often speak in a language different from that of the Bank. The Bank speaks the language of the professionals that contribute to investment projects and programs, such as economists, finance experts and engineers, not that of ethicists and social activists.

5.3 From Efficiency to Poverty

The Bank started out with an almost overwhelming concern with efficiency and sound investment and business practices. Its primary interest was to ensure that projects were well-conceived, economically and financially viable, and operated on a businesslike basis. In the early years, the Bank sought to establish itself as a financial institution recognized by the financial markets and that had to absorb Bank's bonds at a reasonable price.

But it is good to remember that the people who conceived of the Bank and wrote its initial charter were also concerned with the welfare of individuals, their development and full employment. Many of them were inspired by the liberal policies of US President Franklin D. Roosevelt's administration, which, with the British government, was the prime mover at the founding 1944 conference at Bretton Woods, New Hampshire. Those founders included Harry Dexter White, John Maynard Keynes and Edward Bernstein, as well as many from the developing countries, such as Roberto Campos and O. Bulhoes (Brazil), Carlos Lleras Restrepo (Colombia), M. Desai (India), Rodrigo Gomes and Vitor Urquidi (Mexico) and Flip Pazos (Cuba).

The bank sharpened its focus on poverty conditions under the leadership of George Woods (1963-1968), who initiated lending for education and sanitation and began the long journey of professionalizing the Bank s economic work. This work continued during McNamara's management, especially after his 1973 Nairobi speech, signaling the start of the Bank's involvement in battling rural poverty by helping small-scale agriculture. Assistance for urban development followed, including housing, sewerage and sanitation, combined with more intensive attention to urban employment. In these 'new-style' projects, the Bank was prepared to take considerable risks. Subsequent evaluation has shown that these projects often had much smaller rates of return than more traditional projects, such as electricity and transport. During this time the Bank also began broadening its analysis of projects by paying attention to the social value of inputs and outputs, that is, the labor costs of projects for a country. Under this method, the labor costs of projects designed to provide jobs and absorb abundant low-skilled labor would be set at zero, reflecting that the cost for this kind of labor is negligible for the country. The costs of a project employing low-skilled labor would therefore be lower than an alternative project designed to increase efficiency by substituting labor with machines. The low social cost of antipoverty projects would make it easier for the Bank to justify its lending for anti-poverty purposes, thus allowing for poverty effects rather than efficiency alone. The broader conception of project justification is important not only for the operations of the World Bank, but also for other lending institutions and governments. Since project evaluation is the one area where the World Bank has exercised considerable influence on economic thinking around the world.

Unfortunately, the World Bank's attention to poverty declined in the 1980s. The debt crisis which dominated the development scene in this past decade brought a setback in growth and social development and worsened poverty conditions, particularly in Latin America. At the same time, the Bank's economic work and operational stance assigned increasing weight to efficiency in resource a location and outward orientation, and less to fighting poverty In the late 1970s, the Bank began to increase non-profit lending to assist countries in adjusting their economies to the changes in the world economy brought about by the second oil price increase and the consequences of adverse terms of trade, high interest rates and recession in the industrial countries. But in many countries, these structural adjustment loans were associated with an increase in poverty, which once again brought the issue to the foreground.

5. 4   Structural Adjustment Lending

The Bank's charter permits non-project lending only in exceptional circumstances. The adverse impact of the second oil price increase in the late 1970s created unusually difficult conditions for many developing countries. Structural adjustment loans were designed to help countries overcome these adverse conditions by providing quickly disbursing aid that helped smooth cuts in consumption and imports, and at the same time made essential policy changes to adjust to worsening external conditions and overcome domestic inflation and fiscal imbalance. These policies have increased export earnings, improved the internal terms of trade in favor of agriculture (where most labor is employed), freed financial resources for private investment by reducing the government budget deficit, and generally enhanced the growth and efficiency of the economy.

In painstaking ex post facto analysis, the Bank's economists have shown that countries that received adjustment loans and implemented policies associated with these loans generally had better growth performance than other ('non-adjusting') countries. Countries that had the best performance were the exporters of manufactures, such as Brazil, Republic of Korea. Morocco, the Philippines, Thailand, Uruguay and Yugoslavia.

In general, structural adjustment lending was most effective in countries that had an institutional framework for policy reform and a high degree of supply response. To allow for essential institutional changes, a much longer-term perspective was required in low-income countries, particularly in SSA, where growth declined, investment decreased in relation to gross output, and inflation worsened-regardless of whether or not the countries adopted adjust policies. Social indicators (calorie intake, infant mortality, life expectancy, primary school enrollment, etc) in SSA showed no improvement in 1980s. (It is ironic that among the strongest early advocates of structural adjustment lending were economists who also have a strong interest in aid to Africa, where structural adjustment lending encountered the greatest obstacles.)

It is important to realize that poverty eradication, or even alleviation, was not an initial objective of adjustment lending. In reality, the poor, especially in urban areas, suffered from the reductions in social expenditures and from the increase in prices of food and of imports as subsidies were removed and exchange rates adjusted. Reduced spending on primary education will have long-lasting negative effects. With contraction in the public sector, many civil servants were laid off and joined the ranks of the poor. While some rural farmers benefited from higher agricultural incomes, especially if involved in export agriculture, most of Africa's small farmers and poor peasants are in fact outside the export economy and are effectively outside the organized economy to which structural adjustment lending was addressed.

Besides the adverse impact on the poor, structural adjustment lending was criticized for other reasons. In some cases the amount of lending was inadequate to cover minimal balance-of-payments change. Projections of economic effects were often overly optimistic. Design and conditionality were too inflexible in the face of different local and institutional circumstances. In other situations, especially in Africa, it became associated with an adversarial and tutorial approach to countries which were deemed not--committed to essential policy reform.

Some NGOs opposed the World Bank's macroeconomic conditions. These NGOs would like to see the Bank give primary attention to microeconomic essentials, such as human development, job creation, the environment and reduction in military spending. Thus, they would support macroeconomic conditions only to the extent that these conditions help the essential characteristics of development. Macroeconomic conditions can have undesirable side effects; for example, export development can reduce the supply of food for the poor and have unfavorable environmental effects.

In light of these criticisms, the World Bank has sought to redesign its structural adjustment lending. For example, subsidies can be reduced and producer prices raised in a more gradual manner. The consequences for budget expenditures may be compensated for by selective increases in taxation, especially of the wealthy. Social expenditures can be maintained, not cut. when they have a disproportional benefit for the poor, such as medical programs in Korea. Moreover, these expenditures can be targeted toward the poor where this is possible administratively, for example, in Chile. Finally, some countries have undertaken compensatory programs, like small public works in Ghana. Bolivia and Mexico, often with the help of external finance and NGOs. In Senegal, laid-off civil servants have been retrained and relocated.

5.5 From Structural Adjustment to Fighting Poverty

With structural adjustment tending underscoring, if not exacerbating, poverty in recipient countries, the Bank once again focused on poverty issues. The World Development Report 1990 was entirely dedicated to a new poverty-reduction effort that became the center of operations. Bank staff started to undertake country-by-country poverty assessments that ascertain who, were and why of poverty, and to lay the basis for policy discussions with governments. An increasing proportion of   was dedicated to fighting poverty directly.   At the same time, structural adjustment loans were redesigned to make sure they would not adversely affect the poor; some loans were made to improve the delivery of social services to the poorest population groups (for example, the 1994 loan to Zambia).

The Bank's poverty assessments assemble economic and social data that are essential to a dialogue on poverty issues confronting the countries concerned. The exercises identify, from vantage point of the impact on the poor, shortcomings in policy, planning, sector priorities and investments and the delivery of social services. They consider the impact of long-term economic management on the ability of the poor to build up assets as well as the effects that short-term economic measures, inflation and cuts in public expenditures have on the poor.

The Bank s new poverty initiative was accompanied by greater attention to the role of women in development, under the guidance of President Barber Conable (1986-1991). An abundance of facts have made it evident that women suffer the brunt of poverty, so development policies must explicitly address the need for improving the condition of women. The Bank has given greater attention to the education of women, a crucial element in reducing population growth, and to making a higher proportion of loans for human resource development that address women's issues.

These lending operations were guided in part by a program of targeted interventions, loans with the primary objective of poverty reduction, especially for women and children, through basic education, productivity of small farmers, basic health conditions, sanitation and water supply, and basic infrastructure in regions of concentrated poverty. Loans in this category amounted to 12-15 per cent of total lending in 1991 and 1992. Moreover, the Bank's lending for human resource development-education, health, family planning and nutrition-has tripled since the early 1980s and is now 15 per cent of total lending.

While these activities mark a turnaround in the Bank's operational orientation, further policy charges are needed to broaden and widen this program. It is clear, moreover, that anti-poverty lending does not proceed in isolation from the Bank's advice on overall development policies. In

his address to the Bank's 1994 Annual Conference on Development Economics. World Bank Vice President and Chief Economics Michael Bruno, tied together three critical elements in basic development policy:
- attainment of sustained average per capita growth is a necessary condition for sustained reduction in poverty;
- implementation of an adjustment package of policy reform is a necessary condition for sustained per capita growth; and
- fiscal and monetary restraint is a necessary condition for adjustment.

But these necessary conditions are not sufficient. Economic growth must be combined with direct policies targeted at improving conditions for the poor. At the same time, anti-poverty policies require growing public resources for the financing of various measures. Anti-poverty measures are strongly correlated with the ups and downs of economic growth.

5.6 Poverty and the Environment

Environmental policies have opened a new window on anti-poverty action. The poor suffer most from environmental degradation, unclean water and indoor air pollution. Environmental degradation depresses the poor's income by diverting more time to routine tasks, such as collecting firewood, and lowering productivity of natural resources. The poor cannot afford to make investments in natural resources (for example, soil conservation) that produce long-term results. To the contrary, they will tend to overuse resources, as for example the overgrazing of lands in Africa. In Bangladesh, to survive, the poor have deforested the land which in turn has become more prone to flooding.

The Bank was late in helping improve environmental policies and integrating its operations pro-environment activities, and still has a long way to go. Although many environmental economists and some more general economists (like Kenneth Boulding and Herman Daly) have been aware for decades of the shortcomings of conventional economics, until recently they had little impact on the economic analysis used in the World Bank and other lending institutions.

Once environmental considerations are given explicit recognition, no strand of conventional economic reasoning can remain untouched. For example, exports from Indonesia or Cote d'Ivoire of tropical hardwood logs that take centuries to grow must make allowance for depreciation of natural resources. The foreign exchange earned from such exports is not a net gain. More generally, the national accounts must be adjusted downward. They must allow for resource depletion and for the monetary cost of degradation; these two adjustments alone add up to 13 per cent of net domestic product in Mexico. In addition to making explicit allowance for the causes and consequences of environmental degradation, environmental policies can be linked directly with anti-poverty measures: thus, distribution of food during periods of drought can help avoid the overuse of natural resources.

The bank has recently begun to link its operations to the concept of sustainable development. Yet, few environmentalists will be fully satisfied with the work of an institution of the complexity, diversity and size of the World Bank. The Bank's environmental activities cut across many sectors, including agriculture and electric power generation and distribution. As a global institution, it is well suited to deal with many problems of a cross-border nature. It is administering the Global Environment Facility and is managing several environmental programs (for example, for the Mediterranean, Black and Baltic Seas and the Danube River Basin). In conjunction with officials in borrowing countries, the Bank is formulating environmental action plans for individual countries that lay the foundations for discussions on their environmental policies. In the year ending June 1993, it lent $2 billion for 24 projects with a primary environmental objective (that is, projects with over 50 per cent of project costs or benefits for environmental improvements).

5.7   The Bottom Line Is People

The Bank's economic policy analyzes and dialogues often appear far removed from a concern with individuals, although, of course, the recommended economic measures and engineering procedures are presumed to benefit individuals in the end. However, it is easy for a global institution with complex technical operations to overlook its impact on real people, especially the poor. To some extent this shortcoming is being corrected by the work of sociologists in the Bank.

For many years, the Bank has enjoyed social anthropologists to help make individual projects and policy advice more compatible with the interests of people directly affected by the project, especially the poorest, including indigenous peoples. Sociologists point out that a people-based approach can produce results that are fundamentally different from the investment-based and economic policy-based approaches which have been customarily recommended by engineers and economists. They will draw attention to the characteristics of the recipient population, the social organization of people in the project area and the cultural acceptability of the project and its compatibility with the expressed needs and wants of the intended beneficiaries. Following the advice of sociologists, since 1979 the Bank has initiated a policy governing the displacement of people by projects (usually big dams). This policy aims to relocate dislocated people at the same or higher standard of living and assure that the project design reduces actual displacement, as much as possible. (The Bank expects that 2 million people will need to be relocated by its projects over a 10-year period. The Bank's activity represents only a small fraction of what goes on in the world: each year work starts on some 300 big dams in developing' countries that displace around 4 million people, of which the World Bank will fund no more than 3 per cent). The Bank also seeks to ensure that indigenous people do not suffer adverse effects from new investments: projects must allow for their impact on indigenous people and make sure they are compatible with indigenous rights, customs and culture.

Sociologists have also urged the application of participatory investments planning at local community level, as practiced in Mexico's huge rural project. But in an institution dominated by time quantitative professions of economics and engineering, sociologists still have some way to go before they are fully integrated in the Bank's work.

However well-crafted the programs of the World Bank, to be effective they must be governed by the local efforts. The people directly affected by these programs must be the prime movers in initiating and shaping them. Outsiders' advice can at best support and strengthening the efforts of the countries concerned. All essential facilitating measures--education, health and sanitation and social services-must have roots in home soil. Most of the finance for social and infrastructure programs must in any case come from domestic sources.

Moreover, without the personal motivation and commitment by the poor themselves to a program, no design can be fully effective against re my obstacles that must be overcome, most notably the sheer numbers of people seeking improved conditions, and the interests of those groups that want to maintain the status quo. In addition, those who work directly with the poor will understand well the importance of the poor's own motivation and commitment to a program. These people are in fact the critical agents that are able to strengthen the chances for a program's success.

The World Bank, for its part, can intensify its efforts against poverty and provide a broader, long-term perspective and global leadership. To do so will require policy changes in at least three areas:

- The Bank must give its staff more opportunity to concentrate on situations in individual countries so it can be more in tune with the social and cultural diversity of these countries;
- The Bank must formulate a coherent overall strategy for poverty eradication;
- The Bank will need to mobilize adequate resources

for an expanded anti-poverty program which is bound to compete with claims from important programs.

5.8 Dedicate Staff Resources to Fighting Poverty

To be effective in assisting countries in their fight against poverty, Bank staff must have intimate knowledge of these country's culture, institutions, politics and social fabric, as well as the economic and technical ramifications of an anti-poverty program. Staff stationed in resident offices will need to be strengthened and work closely with NGO workers. Staff may have to spend considerable time, even years, working on individual countries or regions to attain an adequate level of knowledge and experience. (Bank personnel management now encourages staff to move to a new assignment after three years, that is, 'move on in order to move up the corporate ladder. This movement may be seen as in the interest of managerial efficiency, but may run contrary to essential staff concentration on individual countries.)

If the Bank is to be serious about fighting poverty in many diverse country situations (or even diverse regions within individual countries), it must encourage interested staff to stay and to attain familiarity that is needed for fighting poverty in ways suitable to the social and economic circumstances and conditions of individual countries. More generally, this kind of country-specific knowledge is also essential for obtaining local participation in project and program preparation and execution.

At present, the Bank's poverty assessments are technically competent reports, but they are highly standardized and make little allowances for countries' cultural and social characteristics. That must change if the Bank is to put flesh on its skeleton models and reach genuine undertakings with the countries concerned and assist them in making the social, political, economic and financial commitments necessary for effective action. The Bank has a strong professional basis for making these changes.

5.9 Towards an Anti-Poverty Strategy

Beginning with the World Development Report 1990, the Bank has done a competent and professional job in studying the dimensions of poverty, indication basic measures to overcome it, mapping out different policy options, instructing staff how to proceed and lay the base for dialogue with member countries. But all this does not add up to an overall strategy; so far, the Bank has refrained from formulating such a strategy.

In this respect, the Bank's poverty reduction program is reminiscent of its lack of a strategy to deal with the debt crisis, which dominated the development scene in the 1980s. In the 1960s, the Bank staff had already constructed a comprehensive theoretical and conceptual framework for dealing with a debt in a development context. It also had the data essential for tracking the debt build-up process, as well as in-depth knowledge of the economic situation of debtor countries, including medium-term projections of their balance-of-payments situation and external indebtedness. Its country analyses gave me Bank and undisputed insight into the nature and seriousness of the debt situation in the 1970s and early 1980s. But instead of laying out a strategy, first for avoiding, and then for overcoming the crisis once it burst upon the development scene, the Bank's management took a back seat. The Bank reacted only to the piecemeal initiatives of other players, mainly the main creditor countries, even though these initiatives did not begin to measure up to the dimensions of the problem as understood by the World Bank economists.

In contrast to its approach to the debt crisis, the Bank has now set out to pursue poverty reduction as a central element of its operations. It has the toots to formulate an overall strategy which can give the world a new vision of what can and cannot be accomplished and can enable the Bank to provide badly needed leadership in this area. At a minimum, an overall strategy would:

- Set forth the objective of eradicating poverty in different types of developing countries and in the countries of Eastern Europe and in the countries of Eastern Europe and the former Soviet Union.
- Specify the policies needed to reach the objective.

— by the countries themselves;
— by the international community, including financial assistance for country programs and investments for overcoming poverty and associated operations in related areas, such as environmental programs of particular interest to the poor; and
— by the industrial countries, particularly in the area of trade.

- Clarify the time frame in which the Bank expects the recipient countries, the industrial countries and international community to work.
- Indicate the resources and sacrifices required to reach the objective on the part of the countries taking action, and in capital, financial and technical resources on the part of the World Bank, other

lenders and bilateral donors.
- Present regular performance progress reports on what lenders, industrial countries and international community, are doing and on what progress is being achieved in poverty eradication. These reports would assess the performance under the Bank's and other programs. Given the comprehensive nature of taking stock of performance in poverty eradication, the Bank, in exercising a catalytic function, may want to obtain cooperation from other institutions. However, it is important that it assures essential leadership in this effort which so clearly falls in its domain.

In the framework of such a broader strategy. anti-poverty criteria should be applied to all the Bank's work, from the formulation of country assistance programs to the selection and design of projects, and be built into project conditions. In this way the Bank's poverty assessments would be carried out for all project undertakings.

5.10 Mobilizing Adequate Financial Resources

The Bank's poverty eradication program will have to compete for resources with other important programs such as the reconstruction and rehabilitation of states in transition from socialism, environmental and infrastructure lending, continued major programs in China, India, Latin America and the Middle East and special new programs in the former Israeli-occupied territories. South Africa and hopefully soon the republics of the former Yugoslavia and the salvation of the Amazonian rain forest. Moreover, poverty eradication will become more ambitious. For example, poverty eradication will have to extend to countries which still have regions with deep-seated poverty even though they have successfully followed policies of stabilization and adjustment. These countries have a greatly strengthened economic and financial base from which to attack poverty, and moreover, attract substantial amounts of private capital. The Bank will have to extend its poverty lending to relevant countries if it is lead a truly comprehensive effort against poverty. In this respect, the anti-poverty program should extend well beyond assistance to the poorest countries.

It is not unreasonable to assure that the Bank will be able to mobilize the resources necessary to undertake a more ambitious anti-poverty program of this kind, and that it will get cooperation from other lenders, both multilateral and bilateral. Given the other claims on its resources, the International Bank for Reconstruction and Development may well have to seek an increase in its capital. Many countries that are creditworthy for IBRD loans are candidates for anti-poverty assistance, both technical and financial, and in countries where poverty rates are o the upper ranges, continued International Development Association financing will be necessary. In the end, many parties will have to collaborate if the global community is to reach the goals of a realistic poverty eradication program.

5.11 Conclusion

Fighting poverty is and should be a primary objective of the World Bank, but it has sometimes been put on the backburner, as in the first haft of the 1980s. This may happen again. Looking ahead, one can only hope that the Bank will persist in objectives of the early 1990s, and will broaden its programs as suggested. Strong and committed leadership will be essential if this is to happen.

Chapter 6

The World Bank and the International Environmental Agenda

6. 1 Introduction

The World Bank was the first of the multilateral development banks to express an interest in environmental consequences of development. The creation of the post of Environmental Adviser in 1970 marked the Bank's first attempt to address environmental issues. The evolution of its environmental policy over the past two decades has been shaped by internal bureaucratic politics and external actor –donor countries, borrowing members and nongovernmental Organizations.

Until the creation of an Environmental Department in 1987, as part of Conable's reorganization of the Bank, environmental concerns were addressed through the Office of Environmental and Scientific Affairs (OESA). This was an inadequately staffed section which focused primarily on assessing the environmental impact of projects. In addition to identifying and preparing environmental projects, OESA's tasks included generating greater awareness inside and outside the Bank about the ecological and resource management impact of development projects; reviewing project implementation in order to assess the environmental consequences; and cooperation with other agencies such as UNDP and UNEP to develop research and operational policy. OESA was given a broad mandate but limited resources with which to implement it.

In a speech to the World Resources Institute in May 1987, Barber Conable acknowledged mistakes in previous Bank environmental policy. He announced a number of organizational reforms and new initiatives designed to increase the effectiveness of the Bank's environmental policy.

A new central Environment Department was established with 30 staff members in three divisions. Its role is to conduct policy and research in technical, economic and social areas, to provide conceptual guidance or specialized expertise for staff in the regional offices, to establish and maintain information systems and databases and to train and educate Bank staff on environmental issues. Environmental units were created in each of the Bank's regional units to review Bank-supported projects and liaise with national officials in identifying more general tasks related to resource management.

6.2 New Initiatives

New initiatives designed to integrate development planning and environmental management follow the suggestions of the Brundtland commission have been taken. A five-year program to conduct in-depth environmental assessments of 30 countries is currently underway. A less detailed but, nevertheless, important environmental statement for each borrowing country, an environmental issue paper, is also in preparation. Furthermore, specific regional projects examining interrelated environmental issues have been undertaken. For example, the Bank is participating in an Environmental Program for the Mediterranean along with UNEP, the European Investment Bank and the Mediterranean countries. And in conjunction with UNDP and the Economic Commission for Asia and the Pacific has embarked on the Capital Cities Clean-up Project to counter the damaging environmental effects of rapid urbanization, industrial pollution and environmental neglect in the main Asian cities.

Since 1987 the Bank has attempted to develop ways of integrating environmental issues into development policy-making. From the Bank's perspective, its lending activities have become much more sensitive to ecological concerns. It has expanded its efforts to address the environmental consequences of aid protects and to identify projects specifically aimed at environmental problems. In 1989, approximately one-third of Bank projects contained significant environmental components. This figure rose to 48 per cent in 1990, remained roughly the same in 1991 but fell back to under 25 per cent in 1992. To assist in the identification of the environmental consequences of a project, in 1990 the Bank developed a fourfold classification of project based on their environmental impacts. A systematic environmental screening of all new projects was introduced in 1990. This enables staff to undertake full environmental impact on assessments on every project with the potential for substantial environmental effects.

Furthermore, from 1989 the Bank began to pay closer attention to the environmental impact of structural adjustment lending. In examining the environmental consequences of project approval and adjustment lending, the Bank is trying to ensure that environmental assessment becomes an inseparable part of its operations. The Bank felt sufficiently confident of its progress on these issues to claim in 1989 that, 'considerable progress was made in fiscal year 1989 in integrating environmental concerns into the mainstream of the Bank operations, policy, research evaluation, training and information activities.'

The preparation of Environmental Issue Papers (EIPs) and EAPs are part of the Bank's strategy to devote explicit attention to environmental issues and to stress the development of policies capable of influencing environmentally related behavior. EIPs are prepared by the Bank and seek to identify key problems and their underlying causes for each borrower. EAPs are prepared by national government, the Bank staff and other external agencies. They aim to provide a framework for integrating environmental considerations into a country's economic and social development programs.

An important source of the Bank's influence in the development aid regime arises from its control over intellectual ideas. The Bank serves as a generator of new ideas on development, new strategies for development and plays an important role in reappraising past experience. The Bank has been in the forefront of the intellectual challenge to investigate the links between the environment and development. The World Bank currently stresses the interdependence between development and environment but this has not always been the case. Early Bank policy tended to prioritize development over the environment. Robert McNamara is quoted as asserting that "There is no evidence that economic growth which the developing countries so desperately require will necessarily involve an unacceptable burden either on their own or anybody's environment."

6.3   Causes of Environmental Degradation

The causes of environmental degradation the Bank are twofold. First, environmental problems can arise from the absence of economic development. Increased population growth in the context of widespread poverty places untold pressure on the land and resources. Environmental problems are arising from the persistence of poverty include poor sanitation and lack of clean water, desertification, devegetation and soil erosion.

Environmental degradation is also, in the Bank's analysis, the consequence of rapid and uncontrolled economic growth. Unfettered urbanization can cause environmental pollution. Air and water pollution is a serious hazard in cities in Africa, Asia and Latin America. From me Bank's perspective a mutually reinforcing link exists between environmental degradation and the development process in three ways: they are caused by a lack of development; they arise from development activities; and they can impair the future development prospects of a country.' The protection of the environment is thus not inimical to development and development need not be harmful to the environment. The influential paper issued in 1987 by the Development Committee of the IMF and World Bank echoed this sentiment in its insistence that, 'Promoting growth, alleviating poverty, and protecting the environment are mutually supportive objectives in the long run.'

6.4 Sustainable Development

The complementarity between the pursuit of development and the preservation of the environment is now reconciled in the concept of sustainable development. Sustainable development, first successfully articulated by the Brundtland Commission, is now accepted by the World Bank as the method by which the goals of development and conservation can be integrated. The Brundtland Commission defined sustainable development as a policy which 'meets the needs of the present without compromising the ability of future generations to meet them own needs.

This record of the evolution of the Bank's environmental policy could be interpreted as an example of a successful process of adaptation to the task environment by the organization. Such an assumption would be unwarranted without a further examination of external pressures on the Bank and a consideration of the views of critics of the Bank's environmental policy.

6.5 Focus of Criticism

The World Bank became the focus of criticism by environmental NGOs and independent analysts in the 1970s and 1980s when it appeared that the Bank disregarded the negative ecological consequences of its project and program lending. The critics accused the Bank of sins of commission and sins of omission. The development by the Bank of policies on issues such as involuntary resettlement (1980), tribal peoples (1982), wildlands (1986) and biodiversity (1986) failed to impress critics who applauded the intentions behind these policies but deplored the lack of specialists and resources to apply such principles effectively to Bank lending policy. World Bank support for colonization schemes such as the Polonoreste project in Brazil and the transmigration project in Indonesia, which contributed to deforestation, came under fierce attack. A number of Bank-financed projects were detrimental to the environment. Bank finance for hydroelectric projects, for example, destroyed watersheds and flooded wildlife sanctuaries and portions of parks in Thailand, Malaysia, Brazil and Zaire. The Bank participated in cattle ranching schemes in Latin America which were destructive of forested areas, and financed a cattle development project in Botswana which contributed to desertification.

These activities produced the image ct an organization willing to sacrifice environmental goals for economic growth. This was further supported by the failure of the Bank to coerce borrowers sufficiently and forcefully to take account of environmental issues and the continuation of projects which had clearly breached the Bank's own environmental guidelines. Even the Bank's attempt to respond to criticism of its forestry policies through the creation in conjunction with the Food and Agricultural Organization (FAO) of a Tropical Forestry Action Plan in 1905 to appease the critics.

The new strategy employed since 1967 is partly a response to the criticisms made by NGOs and others. Bank's much vaunted cooperative stance towards NGOs m this later period is an attempt to stem the flow of criticism as much as a genuine desire for cooperation with major environmental NGOs based in the west, like the International Union for the Conservation of Nature and Natural Resources (IUCN), the World Wide Fund for Nature (WWF) and the World Resources Institute (WRI). It has also sought to engage collaboratively with NGOs based in developing countries.

The Bank's policy has also been shaped in response to the role of international organizations, most notably UNEP, UNDP, FAO, WHO and UNESCO. One result of this collaboration was the creation in 1991 of the Global Environmental Facility (GEF) which is jointly administered by the Bank, UNEP and UNDP. Based on a proposal by France to the Development Committee in 1989, agreement was reached on the establishment of the GEF in November 1990 and it became operational in March 1991. As of June 30, 1992 more than 30 countries were participants in the GEF. Although many developing countries are skeptical of the scheme, nearly half of the participating countries are from the developing world. The developing countries wanted the GEF to be an independent agency, rather than one run by the World Bank, where the dominance of the rich countries over decision-making will be decisive in shaping GEF priorities.

As we have seen, the World Bank's environmental policy addresses a variety of issues, and has been evolving in a positive direction since 1987. However, although it is clear that ecological factors have been included in the Bank's development projects in the recent past there is still considerable room for improvement by the Bank, and convincing grounds to doubt whether the Bank can fulfill its environmental mandate satisfactorily.

The Bank gives the impression that its concern for the environment is internally driven but the evidence suggests that external pressure plays a crucial role. The Bank is particularly sensitive to the demands of the US Congress which, in 1991, threatened to withhold 25% percent of American contribution to the Bank's budget unless the Bank improved its record in implementing environmental reforms in its lending policy. The recent case in which the Bank persisted in its decision to provide financing for Narmada project in India despite a damning report by an independent enquiry set up by the Bank, is a sign that it has not accepted the logic of a genuine ecological perspective on development. This appears to be another example of an inherent flaw in the Bank lending policy.

6.6   Conclusion

The World Bank shows a remarkable ability to adapt to the changing international economic environment. Its preeminent position in the aid regime stems as much from this flexibility, as from its command over financial and intellectual resources. The World Bank is a constantly evolving organization. It has undergone widespread organizational change since its creation at Bretton Woods. Its development strategy also has shifted with changes in the dominant orthodox perception of development. The Bank is not a passive recipient of development thinking; on the contrary, it is in the forefront of research on the causes of and solutions to global poverty. The Bank's unrivalled expertise and resources gives it a very powerful position in the arena of development diplomacy. But, the Bank's relationship with its Third World clients is not a calm and harmonious one.

Third World states welcome the aid provided by the Bank, and recognize that the aid from multilateral organizations like the World Bank have less political strings attached than bilateral aid. Nevertheless, Third World states voice two major criticisms of the Bank and its activities. First, they want to reform the decision-making process in the organization so that it better reflects their views. The dominance of the rich countries, especially the United Sates, over the Bank, shapes its overall approach and affects the level of its funding. The rich countries are unlikely to relinquish control as long as they continue to bear the major cost of direct financing of the organization. Secondly, the developing countries resent the application of conditionality to Bank loans. This is both an issue of principle and one of substance. The discussion of adjustment lending showed that many borrowing countries are either unwilling or unable to implement the Bank recommendations. This highlights a major flaw in the design of Bank projects and programs, and the fact that recipient governments are not pawns of the Bank. The leverage the Bank exercises will vary on an individual basis. The Bank is a reformist organization and judgment on its role in meeting the needs of the Third World will differ depending on whether one accepts the reformist goals of the organization. The Bank has adapted to changes in the global political economy but it has done so within a framework determined by its organizational ideology and the interests of the leading donor states. The main objective of the Bank remains the 'goal of modernizing the international economy in its capitalist variant for the sake of its long term preservation.' Widespread disagreement exists on the extent to which that goal is compatible with promoting economic development and reducing poverty in Third World countries. The development strategies pursued by most Third World elites in the post-World War II period reveals a willingness to accept the basic premise on which the World Bank was established, even if disagreement exists on precise policies to be adopted.

Chapter 7

Innovation of the World Bank's Work and Challenges Ahead

7. 1　Innovative Work of the World Bank

Among all international organizations, the World Bank is probably the agency which has experienced the most varied and profound changes and innovations in its activities over the years. The pace of such changes has particularly increased in the decades of the eighties and the beginning of nineties under the managements of A.W. Clausen and Barber B. Conable, successive presidents of the World Bank Group in this period. Yet, the basic legal documents governing the work of the World Bank Group have remained practically unchanged, except for the creation of a new affiliate, the Multilateral Investment

Guarantee Agency (MIGA) in the late eighties. In fact, the Articles of Agreement of the IRRD, the oldest of the institutions, have not been amended since their adoption in 1944, except on two occasions. In 1965, the IBRD's Articles were amended for the first time to enable it to lend to its first established affiliate, the International Finance Corporation (IFC), and in 1989, they were amended again only to increase the voting power needed for their further amendment by the Bank's members, following approval by its Board of Governors, from 80% of the total votes to 85%. The latter amendment has had the effect, at least in theory, of making the amendment process an even more cumbersome one.

The difficulties in adapting old legal texts to changing circumstances are well known and have been dealt with in every legal system through interpretation and the filling of gaps by courts and legal scholars. In the case of the IBRD and its affiliates, the Board of Executive Directors is entrusted with the task of interpreting the Articles when a question arises and its decision in this respect are subject only to review by the Board of Governors upon the request of a Bank member. In the early practice of the IBRD, many formal interpretations were issued. No formal interpretation has been made since 1964, with the single exception of a 1986 Board decision on the standard of value of the IBRD capital.

There is no doubt that the activities of the IBRD and its affiliates have changed over the years and are likely to experience further variations as the world with which they deal changes.

The IBRD was originally envisaged as a complementary source of finance, mainly for the foreign exchange cost of specific reconstruction or development projects. It was intended to assume this role primarily through the issuance of guarantees to private lenders and participation in their loans, and to provide direct loans only when its borrowers were otherwise unable to borrow from the market on reasonable terms. Another possible role envisaged for the IBRD as an exception in "special circumstances" was to provide finance for other than specific projects as might be needed to achieve its purposes. This early vision has however proved to be narrower than, if not different from, what actually happened. The IBRD's earliest loans financed general imports, not specific projects; its first guarantee was made late in 1984 and its participation in private loan syndicates was pursued for a while only after 1983. A broader approach towards the financing of social projects and of local costs generally has been followed since the late l960s. In the l970s, the Bank, recognizing that development is a broader concept than growth, introduced an emphasis on income distribution. The Bank's present role in supporting policy reform through adjustment loans, initiated in 1980, was also not envisaged as such at the time of the drafting of the Articles. In the late l980s, further changes were introduced, including lending for debt and debt service reduction and free standing environment loans.

In taking up such innovations, the Bank has not resorted to the amendment of its charter. It has been able to innovate through policy changes and practical measures. In doing so, however, it has been careful not to depart from explicit requirements in its Articles and not to act outside its legally authorized powers. In this respect, its readings of the meaning of these Articles have accorded primary attention to their ultimate objective and the overall mandate of the institution as a financier of investment for productive purposes in reconstruction or development efforts, and as a facilitator of international investment and trade.

7.2 Challenges Ahead

The World Bank's experience over the years, coupled with its access to financial resources and information, have clearly made it the international institution best equipped to deal with the complexities of development issues.

However, it will continue to face challenges which, whether they are of an economic, social or environmental nature, wilt involve a host of conflicting interests. These are not limited to the typical conflicts between public and private, rural and urban, national and global, or immediate and medium term concerns but extend to a broad array of other issues including intergenerational ones where trade-offs constantly have to be made between the interests of present and future generations.

It is dear that countries with better economic policies and investment climates stand to gain more in the competition for the scare resources of the world. The World Bank has an added challenge in assisting its borrowing members not to lose out in such as competition and in making sure that the poorest countries will not be further marginalized in the process.

In facing the challenges of development, the World Bank is increasingly aware that its battle is, and should continue to be, a battle against poverty. Freedom from poverty does not only allow people to raise their materials standards of living, it is a basic foundation of all forms of human progress, including the enjoyment of human rights and the protection of the environment.

Chapter 8

The World Bank in the New Century

Message From the Chairman of the Board of Executive Directors

A new millennium is beginning. Foe World Bank, it is a time to ask ourselves, how can we improve our effectiveness in the fight against poverty? It is also a time to act: with urgency and with responsibility. Urgency, because roughly two billion more people will be joining us on the planet in the next 25 years, and we must be ready for them. Responsibility, because the 2.8 billion poor who currently live on less than two dollars a day are our fellow human beings, and not just a statistic.
Achieving a world free of poverty is an enormous and complex undertaking. And solutions are far from simple. The challenges are multidimensional; they call for people,

groups, and institutions to come together to play a wide range of roles in a collegial, collective effort. It is only with strong coalitions-local, national, regional, and global-that we will succeed in fighting poverty; that much is clear. What does it take to reduce poverty?

Our strategy, at the country level, is rooted in a wealth of lessons from development experience. Some of the key lessons are that development assistance leads to progress in sound policy and institutional environments; that economic growth is crucial to but must be accompanied by government action targeted to meet poor people's needs and to address the social cost of reform; that the reforms cannot be imposed from the outside but must be "home-grown"; that communities must have a voice and play a role in their own development; that open economies grow faster than closed economies. Our recent work on poverty-economic analysis as well as consultations with poor people – reveals that people in poverty are an asset, not a liability. It is imperative that we give them opportunities, that we empower them, and that we ensure their security.

Drawing on these lessons, our work is guided by the following principles:

- Country ownership: A country's progress depends fundamentally on its directing the policy agenda. Actions taken without broad buy-in have too often turned out to be unsustainable. Success requires that consensus-building by all stakeholders be part of the action agenda.
- Long-term integrated approach: To achieve sustainable growth, crucial for poverty reduction, poverty reduction strategies must be multidimensional. These strategies must address

macroeconomics as well as social, environmental, and institutional needs, progress must occur on all fronts, ranging from governance, anticorruption, and judicial and financial systems to health, education, and transport policies.
- Partnership: Collaborative relationships, shared objectives, and a mutually agreed-upon division of labor are crucial. We need to go beyond aid coordination: we need to align strategies, be selective, draw on mutual expertise, and reduce wasteful competition and duplication among donors.
- Result Focus: It is crucial to have development outcomes as our guides, and these must flow directly from the long-term vision. Countries must set poverty reduction targets, lay our public policy actions to achieve them, and work with civil society to monitor progress.

We put forward this vision last year to the global community under a pilot approach we call the Comprehensive Development Framework (CDF). I am heartened that it is increasingly a shared vision. More countries and more partners are testing the CDF approach and participating in this work-in-progress. Our work with these countries in fiscal 2000 has advanced: their interest creates the learning ground, their experience will define the way forward. Continuing this theme is our joint endeavor with the IMF to help those countries eligible for debt relief, under the Heavily Indebted Poor Countries (HIPC) Initiative, to produce Poverty Reduction Strategy Papers (PRSPS). Our strategy to fight poverty also requires action at the global level. There is much that can be done to promote disease reduction globally through greater use of cost-effective vaccines; to raise awareness of the impact of HIV/AIDS on development; to address transnational challenges such as the prevention of financial crises; to provide concerted debt relief to poor countries; and to preserve the world's natural resources.

Each of these efforts could have a profound impact on poverty. In addition, empowering people with knowledge and technology could have far-reaching benefits. The Bank has taken important steps to advance the concept of the "Knowledge Bank", including efforts to develop the framework for a Global Development Gateway, being conceived as an Internet-based vehicle facilitating the provision and exchange of information.

At both country and global levels, our emphasis is on demand-driven services and aid effectiveness. The past year's decline in lending relative to the previous year's record volume attests to this evolution. Emerging market countries have needed substantially less financial support due to the strong recovery of global financial markets and a resumption of access to private capital. Other countries are indeed in need but lack the circumstances (national peace as well as sound policies and institutions) that would permit an effective use of financial aid. Lower lending also reflects small-sized operations, through which the "New Bank" has responded to country needs and adopt pilot approaches and build institutional capacity as prerequisites to successful development efforts. The Bank has, moreover, increased its reliance on non-lending services in the policy dialogue, recognizing their key role in building support for development efforts.

I cannot stress enough the importance of partnerships.

The task ahead is too formidable for and single institution or set of institutions to tackle. Everyone of us has a role to play: private sector, public sector, civil society, nongovernmental organizations, academia, religious groups, multilateral and bilateral donors, and development organizations. If we are to achieve the United Nations-based inter- national development targets, we all need to work together. Halving poverty levels by 2015 is possible, but only if we concert our efforts in a new way.

It is my firm conviction that the Bank has a crucial role to play in this challenge. As a cooperative, we enjoy the backing of nearly every nation of to world in pursuing our mission. As a development institution with a half-century of experience across countries and sectors, we have a vast array of lessons that we continue to build m every day. As a global institution with offices throughout the world, we have an unparalleled reach, growing in leaps and bounds in this age of communication, which is helping us get closer to the people we serve, and to share knowledge that is key to empowerment and progress. As a strong financial institution and leader in capital markets, we mobilize funding on good terms and tailor it to meet long-term development needs typically unmet by private creditors. And as a multinational employer, we are blessed with a rich pool of skills and talent, a group of people with an unequaled professionalism and devotion to fighting against poverty. I am enormously indebted to them.

The World Bank's track record shows clearly that we are making a difference, and that we are learning and adapting to client needs. Our task is to build on all that we have achieved. We, as a global community, can go down the business-as-usual path and see the numbers of poor grow steadily, decade after decade; or we can innovate and follow the path with more unknowns but infinitely more promise. For the Bank the choice is clear: we have embarked on a path of change, and we are committed to listening, learning, and acting in partnership until more and more people partake in the many opportunities that the new era of growth, technology, and global development has to offer.

Appendix

The World Bank in China

China rejoined the World Bank in May 1980. The Bank made its first loan to China in 1981 in support of the development of Chinese universities. Over the years, the relationship between China and the World Bank Group has grown into a mature and significant partnership for development. World Bank commitments to China by June 30, 2000 exceeded US$34 billion for a total of 226 projects. About half of these projects are still under implementation, making China's portfolio by far the largest in the Bank. World Bank-supported projects can be found in all the major sectors of the economy and most of provinces, municipalities and autonomous regions across China. Infrastructure (transport, energy, industry, urban development) accounts for more than half of the total portfolio and agriculture, social sectors (health, education, social protection), environment and water supply and sanitation comprise the remainder. All these have a direct or indirect impact on poverty alleviation. China is also one of the Bank's best performing member countries in terms of project implementation.

In addition to financial assistance, the provision of non-financial services in the form of technical assistance, policy advice, workshops and training is an essential part of the cooperation program. Through such services, the Bank assists the Chinese government in implementing its policies for reducing poverty, for macroeconomic management and for structural reforms by bringing international experience and best practices from around the world and helping build up local institutional and technical capacities.

The current World Bank Group's assistance strategy is designed to assist China to meet its objectives in the four key areas of the country's development agenda:

- public sector management and accountability including macroeconomic management, fiscal and monetary policy and related areas of structural reforms;
- transitions to a socialist market economy including the establishment of the legal, institutional and regulatory framework, financial sector reform, state-owned enterprise reform and private sector development, investment in people, and development of supportive infrastructure;
- rural development to improve rural incomes and welfare,
- increase agricultural productivity, develop and manage water resources, and improve natural resources management and environmental protection; and

- urban development to improve urban development planning and management, implement the reform of housing, land and labor markets, including the development of improved social safety nets, and protect the urban environment.

The World Bank's China program is managed through its office in Beijing, which today comprises of more than 90 international and local staff. The Bank's counterpart agency in China is the Ministry of Finance, which takes prime responsibility for the formulation and implementation of the World Bank assistance programs in China.

(The End)

www.ingramcontent.com/pod-product-compliance
Lightning Source LLC
Chambersburg PA
CBHW070205230526
45471CB00002B/835